THE GOLFERS DICTIONARY

FUNNY FUNNY DEFINITIONS!! *(A PERFECT LIE)*

By Martin A. Ragaway
and The Editors
of Funny
Funny
World

Illustrations by René Rembrand

PRICE STERN SLOAN
Los Angeles

EIGHTH PRINTING—MARCH 1988

Copyright © 1984 by Martin Ragaway
Published by Price Stern Sloan, Inc.
360 North La Cienega Boulevard, Los Angeles, California 90048

ISBN: 0-8431-0988-2

PREFACE

Ah! you may say, A Golfer's Dictionary. Do We Really Need It? you may say, thinking that those of us who play this odd game are already aware of the technical nomenclature, the appropriate expletives and the inappropriate excuses which are necessarily included in the vocabulary of the well rounded Golfist.

On the other hand, if you (presumptive purchaser and reader of this book) do not play golf you may say, Why Do I Need It?

Well! I say. This book you hold in your hand, or (if you have a very, very successful marriage, this book that your spouse is holding up for you to see) is not meant to be instructional. It is not presented as an aid to the twenty-five handicap duffer. It is designed solely to amuse you whether you do, or do not, play the Big Game.

We have here a comic overview of America's second most popular participatory game. It won't improve your backswing or tighten up your short game, but it is Fun. Which is more than a lot of us can say about our golf game.

Roger T. Price
("Boomer" to his friends
at The Shadow Hills Pitch 'n' Putt)

Ace:

A hole-in-one. There are four in every deck of cards, but none in the lives of most golfers.

Addressing the ball:

Preparation before starting a stroke that'll land your ball in the rough. When you address the ball be sure to put on your Zip code.

Advice:

A golfer can accept advice gracefully—if it doesn't interfere with what he intended to do in the first place.

Addressing the ball

Ambience

Alibi:

An unacceptable excuse for a lousy drive offered by someone other than yourself.

Allergy:

Hypersensitivity to pollen or dust. A defense against those who say your game is nothing to sneeze at.

Ambience:

Found in a golf club were the dues are twice as much as at one that just has atmosphere.

American know-how:

Figuring out the best buy in Japanese-made clubs.

Approach:

On the course, a medium or short iron shot. Off the course: "Honey, you can't believe how lonely it is to be rich and not married."

Atheist:

A fellow in a foursome with a minister, a priest and a rabbi who won't concede a two-inch putt.

Atheist

Ball

B

Backside:

Second nine holes on an 18 hole course. Also, the first thing you notice in a tight pair of jeans.

Bad habits:

Something you can't help doing, like letting the club pro relieve you of money when he should be relieving you of your slice.

Ball:

The round object struck by the club. The USGA golf ball is 1.68 inches in diameter, weighs 1.62 ounces and costs about $1.50. By the time you're rich enough to lose one without crying you're too old to hit it that far.

Ball washer:

Either a water tank with brushes or a Siamese tomcat.

Bargain:

A pair of slacks that goes on sale at the Pro Shop the day after you bought them at the regular price.

Beach:

Any sand hazard in which you're trapped. When you total up your strokes, you are entitled to exclaim "sum of a beach."

Ball washer

Birdie

Benefit of the doubt:

What other players give you when they can't see where your ball landed. Also known as blind faith or charity.

Bermuda:

Grass used on courses in the South. When it comes to watching balls sink out of sight, golfers have their own Bermuda Triangle.

Birdie:

One stroke under the designated par. Try to hit a birdie before one hits you.

Bisque:

A handicap stroke an opponent may use at his own discretion on any hole he chooses, although he must so declare before teeing off on that hole. Save the bisque till you're in the soup.

Blind bogey:

A competition in which a score is pulled out of a hat and the player coming closest, wins. If you pull out 7¼ it doesn't count.

Blowhard:

A club member whose mouth saves you the trouble of finding out for yourself how wonderful he is.

Blowhard

Borneo

Bore:

An acquaintance who isn't interested in hearing how well you did yesterday.

Borneo:

Home of many excellent golf courses. Also cannibals. No need for apprehension unless your caddy bastes you with A-1 Sauce.

Bowling:

A sport that, unlike golf, allows you to start and finish with the same ball.

Bridge:

If you play bridge and golf as if they were only games, you're as well adjusted as you're ever going to be.

Buddy:

A fellow who can remember every shot you missed but doesn't bother to remind you.

Bunker:

A depression usually covered with sand. The original bunkers in Scotland were holes that protected sheep against strong winds. Golfers know that Hitler wasn't the first guy to get killed in one.

Bunker

Caddy

C

Caddy:

A person who carries a player's clubs and often keeps score. A good one understands that less is more.

Casual water:

Any temporary accumulation of water, snow or ice. Time out for the john is not considered casual water.

Catering truck:

A rolling restaurant often found on public courses. Warning: if bad food makes your face turn green, other golfers may tee off from your head.

Cautious compliments:

"That was a pretty good shot—in its own way."

Celebrity:

A lousy golfer who gets to play in a lot of tournaments nonetheless.

Celebrity match:

Where everybody is somebody, so nobody is anybody.

Chairman of the board:

An executive who makes split-second decisions at the office which his subordinates will straighten out while he's on the golf course.

Celebrity

Chip shot

Charity tournament:

A philanthropic event. A fun way to help the less fortunate—as long as it is tax deductible.

Charley horse:

A misguided muscle. A stiffness that won't do Charley or anybody else any good.

Chip shot:

A short approach of low trajectory. Also an insult by an Italian. That's a cheapa shot.

Choke:

To grip farther down on the handle. To collapse under pressure. Also, what you do to an opponent who beats you by one stroke.

Class:

Demonstrated not by whether you win or lose, but by how you tear up your scorecard.

Club:

Weapon used to hit ball. Most are made of anger-resistant steel.

Class

Cockamamie course

Club directors:

A group that keeps minutes and wastes hours.

Club pro:

Man who earns a living selling lessons while patronizing his pupils.

Cockamamie course:

Terrain so uneven that when you hit downhill the ball rolls back and hits your ankle.

Committee meeting:

Like a game of golf. You go around for hours and end up where you started.

Congenital liar:
Someone who has time for bridge and fishing as well as golf.

Constructive criticism:
Advice you give another player—whether he wants to hear it or not.

Conversation:
Small talk between shots. If your partner's talking about someone who isn't around, it's gossip. If he's talking about himself, it's dull. If he's discussing your 250-foot drive, it's of paramount importance.

Constructive criticism

Crowding the ball

Courage:

Playing a municipal golf course on Sunday without an anesthetic.

Creative golf:

Flubbing your shots with such precision that your boss will actually believe he beat you fair and square.

Crowding the ball:

Standing too close to the ball can be embarrassing—especially after you've swung at it.

D

Dedication:

A quality epitomized by the man whose mind is occupied with nothing but golf. "Did you know that Ferdinand Magellan went around the world in 1521?"
"That isn't too many strokes when you consider the distance."

Deep in the weeds:

When you're so far out in the rough the club secretary asks you to fill out a change of address card.

Deep in the weeds

Divot

Devout golfer:

Man who prays with an interlocking grip.

Dining room:

Where the only honest words you'll hear are "Waiter, bring me a glass of water."

Diogenes:

If he came back today looking for an honest man, he could skip the golf courses.

Divot:

A piece of turf cut out by a club head during a bad stroke. As a rule, the ball should go farther than the divot.

Dog-leg:

A bend in the fairway either to the right or left. Why is it that the shots always bend wrong?

Dormie:

When a player or side is as many holes ahead as remain to be played in a match. Opponents must win every remaining hole to tie. A dormie is also a college roommate of the opposite sex.

Driving off the tee:

A careful, deliberate swing inevitably followed by the phrase "Aw shit!"

Dormie

Dunk

Duffer:

A golfer who is not having as much fun on Sundays as his wife thinks he is.

Dunk:

To hit a ball into a water hazard. Easier than slamming a doughnut into a cup of coffee.

Eagle:

Two strokes under the designated par. As rare as the bird of the same name.

Eighteen holes:

A long, slow walk punctuated by occasional moments of optimism but generally characterized by crushing disappointment.

Equality:

All golfers are born equal but Arnold Palmer managed to outgrow it.

Eagle

Executive—high powered

Executive:

A guy who talks business on the golf course and golf at his business.

Executive—high powered:

A person who calls his office on his remote phone every five holes to make sure his employees haven't left for the day.

Experience:

What ten years of play gives you. Usually known as *bitter experience*.

Expert:

When you're positive you know what you're doing. Eventually, of course, another expert will write a book proving you *don't* know what you're doing.

Explode:

Hitting out of a sandtrap and taking large quantities of sand with the shot. Also a temper tantrum as the player swears to give up the game. When he calms down he goes right on playing.

Explode

Fantastic day

Fabulous shots:

Other golfers, experiences, like other people's kids, are more difficult to appreciate than your own.

Fairway:

Well kept portion of ground between tee and putting green. We include this because many golfers have never seen it.

Fantastic day:

When everything in your game goes right. But it's not perfect unless someone else in your foursome screws up.

Fashion:

Never wear a madras plaid Nehru jacket, even though a golf course is a place where adults wear clothing they would be ashamed to wear any other place on earth.

Finesse:

What you think you have until you add up your card.

Flag:

A movable marker in the hole on each green. In deference to your game the flag should always be flown at half mast.

Fashion

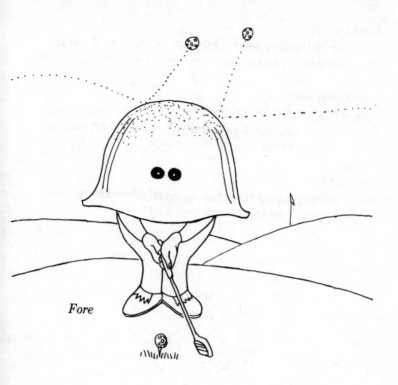

Fore

Flog:

Golf spelled backwards. A reminder of what you really do to yourself.

Fore:

A call used to warn those in danger of being hit with the ball. From the British "Look out before . . ." Do not use if playing with auctioneers. If you say "fore" they will say "I have four. Do I hear five?"

Forthright golfer:

One who turns in a completely accurate scorecard 25 percent of the time.

Found ball:

An extra ball discovered while you're playing. It cannot be considered a found ball until it stops rolling.

Four letter words:

Game! Golf! Putt! Hole! Club! Flag! Ball! Cart! Sand! Trap! Brag! These common four letter words inevitably lead to even *more* common four letter words.

Foursome:

Four friends playing together, each of whom thinks the other three could stand improvement.

Found ball

Fried egg

Free afternoon:

It takes an exclusive country club to show you how expensive a free afternoon can be.

Fried egg:

When the ball is buried in the sand. Don't get hard-boiled about it. Keep your sunny side up.

Fringe:

Grass area that immediately borders the putting surface. Also called the apron, and you *know* how easy it is to mess up an apron.

Fundamentals:

Remember to keep your head down, especially when your boss kicks his ball out of the sand trap.

Fund raiser:

Regular events held to save the club from bankruptcy. Even if *you* aren't in the hole, the club always is.

Fundamentals

Gimme

Generosity:

Remarkable unselfishness which enables a golfing buddy to lend you his car, his condo, his wife, but not his clubs.

Gimme:

A putt so short and inconsequential that it will most likely never be conceded by an opponent.

Goggle:

A boldly hit putt that somehow goes into the hole. It is often done by a turkey.

Golf elbow:

Twinges in the hinges.

Good friend:
Anyone who doesn't play as well as you do—and does it consistently.

Graphite shaft:
Newest luxury in golf clubs that enables you to hit further out of bounds.

Green:
The putting surface which contains the hole or the cup. Also, what it takes a lot of to join the club.

Green

Grounds committee

Gross:

A player's score before his handicap is deducted. Also, your opinion of his game.

Grounds committee:

A duly elected group which dedicates itself to one ultimate goal. Neglect.

Ground under repair:

Any portion of the course so marked by the committee. Do not feel guilty. Your divots had nothing to do with it.

Group behind:

Foursome behind you. They creep up on you like cheap underwear.

Guilt:

Putting down your score and then wiping your fingerprints off the pencil.

Guilt

Handicap

Handicap:

The number of strokes a player receives to adjust his scoring ability. The golf course is the only place where a handicap is not a handicap.

Hanging lie:

A ball resting on a downhill slope. Anyone who claims to have shot under 30 on the back nine at Pebble Beach is telling a lie for which he *should* be hanged.

Happiness:

The feeling a golfer gets from remembering his good shots. Most golfers experience very little of this.

Hazard:

Any bunker or water hazard. Many have been designed by the late Robert Trent Jones, whose apparent wish was that you will hate him after he's gone.

Hell:

Home of the most magnificent golf course you've ever seen, complete with top line pro clubs, all gratis. But not a single golf ball. That's the hell of it.

Hazard

Hole

Hindsight:

Intuitiveness of a well-built woman golfer who knows that if she wears tight shorts, her opponents may not give the game their undivided attention.

Hole:

A round receptacle in the green, four inches in diameter. The golf hole is the only thing in nature that gets smaller as you get closer to it.

Hole-in-one:

A mixed blessing that brings joy and frustration. For the rest of your life you'll never be able to do better on that particular hole.

Hook:

A shot which goes to the left. Once hit by William F. Buckley, who was so embarrassed he immediately gave up the game.

Humility:

This word is not in the golfer's dictionary.

Hypnotist:

A hypnotist can put you in a deep trance and correct your swing. But while you're asleep he steals your starting time.

Humility

Hypochondriac

Hypochondriac:

A non-golfer who joins the country club because it's the only place he can find a doctor on Wednesday afternoon.

Impediments:

Physical handicaps that can make a golfer quit. Example: Harry, who was 83, shot a great game of golf but his eyesight was going and he couldn't see where he hit the ball. He was advised to take Sam with him. Sam could no longer hit the ball but his eyes were perfect. Harry hit the ball and turned to Sam, "Did you see where the ball went?"

Sam said, "Exactly."

Harry: "Where is it?"

Sam: "I forget."

Income tax:

Democracy in action. Income tax gives those who don't play golf an opportunity to lie.

FORM 1040

Golfers - Take your estimated tax and multiply by your handicap. Then double this amount. Remember, you will be audited!

Income tax

Incompetent

Incompetent:

Golfer who hits the ball more on the first hole than others do in 18.

Inconsistency:

The name of the game. One day you go out and top the ball, slice it, hook it, shank it, make all the traps and miss all the greens. And yet, the very next day you go out there and you're really lousy.

Insincerity:

Words that permit you to assure another golfer that his game is as good as he thinks it is.

Instruction:

There is no golf lesson so simple that it cannot be misunderstood.

In the leather:

In friendly matches a player may concede a putt that lies no farther from the cup than the length of the leather wrapping on the other player's putter. Also, standard uniform for S and M golfers.

Intuition:

At times it can be shared by two people: the duffer who knows exactly what equipment he needs and the golf shop salesman who knows exactly how much the duffer can afford to pay for it.

In the leather

Irons

Invention:

The mother of necessity. If you put an eraser on those little short pencils, everyone would be eligible for the club championship.

Irons:

Clubs with metal heads. Long irons are 1, 2, 3. Middle irons are 4, 5, 6. Short irons are 7, 8, 9 and the wedge. All of them can cause you agony. Perhaps someday they'll be made out of painless steel.

J

Joy:

When someone says something nice about your short game before the eulogy.

Joy

Keeping your head down

Keeping score:

Put erasers on those little pencils and you'll have a club full of champions.

Keeping your head down:

The most important rule in addressing the ball. Permits you to hit the ball and pray at the same time.

Knowledge:

What you learn on the links by experience. Mostly things you really don't want to know.

L

Last will and testament:

Final request. One golfer wanted to be buried on his golf course so he could enjoy the hell his friends were still going through.

Lie alike:

Players who have taken the same number of strokes. Also, when your caddy backs up what you say.

Long game:

Shots where considerable distance is important. A match you are hopelessly losing is a *very* long game.

Long game

Loose impediments

Loose impediments:

Natural objects that adhere to the ball, such as twigs, pebbles, leaves, insects and dung. Think of the dung as merely an impediment and not a comment on your game.

Lost ball:

The quickest way to find a lost ball is to put a new one into play.

Luck it:

To drop a putt you didn't expect to make. If your partner does it, he lucks it. If *you* do, it's touch.

Manufacturer's rep:

If he can't break 80 he has no business on the golf course.
If he *can* break 80 he has no business.

Masochist:

A pro who has deluded himself into thinking he can
actually improve your game.

Mistakes:

The natural condition of a hacker's game. The remedy is
to accept these misfortunes like a man. Get a new pro.

Masochist

Moral victory

Moral victory:

Finding a better ball than the one you lost.

Mulligan:

A second shot, usually off the first tee, that is sometimes permitted in a casual social game. Also known as a Shapiro, but only in unrestricted country clubs.

N

Naivete:

The assumption that you're going to be using the same ball after 18 holes of golf.

Near miss:

When you shank the ball out of bounds and it bounces off a Buick and rolls into the gutter, where it is picked up by a nearsighted crow, who then flies over the green and drops it within six inches of the cup. That's when you say "Damn! Another near miss."

Needle:

Gibing an opponent. Causing him to choke or agree to an outrageous bet. If your opponent offers to wager his wife do not accept. (This does not apply if your opponent is John Derek.)

Near miss

Net

Nerves:

A golfer has 45 miles of nerves in his body, and every inch of them stiffens up when he hits the ball.

Net:

A player's score after his handicap is subtracted. Also, what they use to take him away in when he misses a two-inch putt for the match.

Never up, never in:
A rule for hesitant putters. If the ball is not hit hard enough it can't go in. The phrase may also apply to the player's love life.

Nineteenth hole:
The only hole in the course where you can sink an olive.

Nineteenth hole

Obstacles

Obstacles:

Bunkers, sand traps, water holes but most of all, you.

Obstruction:

Anything artificial of any proportion blocking the course. Anyone who addresses the ball for more than 30 seconds may be declared an obstruction.

Off game:

Arnold Palmer's game can be off. Yours is just plain lousy.

Old golfers:

Are not afraid to die. It's just one more hole.

Open stance:

The left foot is dropped behind the imaginary line of the direction of the ball, enabling the golfer to face where he wants to hit. The danger is that if he puts his right foot forward, he'll be hitting where he just came from.

Out of bounds:

The grounds outside the course from which play is prohibited. Take a one stroke penalty. On certain African courses, out of bounds is where the lions are. (Lions hate golf but think golfers are delicious.)

Overclubbing:

Using a club which gives more distance than you need. Not to be confused with bidding problems in tournament bridge.

Out of bounds

ⓟ

Penalty stroke

Palm Springs:

City of a hundred golf courses. If you plan ahead, it's possible to reach the Arizona border without leaving a fairway.

Penalty stroke:

A stroke added for violation of the rules. First introduced by Captain Bligh of the Bounty.

Philosophical:

An attitude of calm about your game which occurs only when you're not playing for money.

Playing through:

Permission to pass requested by players behind to a group ahead of them. It is not advisable to make this request in the john.

Pole one:

To hit a long shot. Also, phrase used by his intimates to address His Holiness, John Paul.

Polyester:

The "natural" fabric for all golfers' clothes. It stays in shape even if its wearer doesn't.

Polyester

Pro shop

Preferred lie:

Local rules which permit a player to improve the position of his ball, without penalty. Also, offering your partners two alibis and seeing which one they go for.

Promising golfer:

Any younger player who listens attentively to your advice and nods his head in agreement.

Pro shop:

Only place in the world where you can buy a purple tam, pink and green checked slacks, and an orange shirt embroidered with blue palm trees, and still be considered the conservatively dressed member of your foursome.

Pro tournament:
One of the few jobs in which the less work you do, the more money you get.

Push:
A controlled shot against the wind, using the wind to bring the ball into the desired line. Weak players are advised to wear a catcher's mask when attempting this shot.

Putt:
The shortest shot which takes the longest time.

Putting green:
The open ground around the hole. It is highly embarrassing to lose a ball on the green.

Push

Quitting golf

Quitting golf:

In order to be smart enough to quit golf, you had to be dumb enough to start.

Referee:

An official appointed by the rules committee. He takes great pains to give them to everyone else.

Refrigeration theory:

Golf balls will last longer if kept in a refrigerator. They will last longer only if never taken out of the refrigerator.

Relaxed:

The only way to hit good shots. Unfortunately, everything about the game is designed to keep you from relaxing.

Refrigeration theory

Rough

Retirement:

When the whole point of your day is to get the figure on your golf score as low as the one on your Social Security check.

Ringer score:

The cumulative scores of a player's lowest number of strokes per hole, set on a given course over a given period of time. Misery on the installment plan.

Rough:

Tall grass off the fairway. If you're hopelessly lost, just take out your putter and hold it above your head. Someone will arrive to advise you what to do next.

Rub of the green:

Euphemism for "tough luck" or "that's the way the ball bounces." If it costs you money, that's *really* the rub of the green.

Rumor factory:

The clubhouse, where everyone knows whose check is good and whose marriage isn't.

Rub of the green

S

Sandtraps

Salesman:

A golfer who can convince his wife that 18 holes is more exercise than mowing the lawn. He hates to play but the doctor is making him do it.

Sandtrap:

Where a duffer spends so much time he should have brought a beach blanket and suntan lotion.

Scorecard:

When blank: an innocent piece of paper.
When filled: a blankity, blank, blank . . .

Scoring lines:

Corrugation on the face of irons designed to guide the ball. For further definition see: Approach.

Scratch player:

One who receives no handicap allowance. For the rest of us, the handicap is coming up with the scratch for the monthly dues.

Scoring lines

Scuffing

Scuffing:

Hitting the ground behind the ball. Although scuffing saves wear and tear on the ball, it's still like slowly digging your own grave.

Self-effacing:

The golfer who can fake being humble after making a great shot.

Shaft:

Part of the club that is not the head. Also, what you get if you're suckered by a golf hustler.

Slice:

A shot that curves to the right. Some golfers never conquer it. Like the New Yorker going to Dallas who wanted his travel agent to book him through Chicago and Los Angeles. Said the agent, "Why not go direct?" To which the golfer replied, "What , with *my* slice?"

Snake:

A very long putt, usually over several breaks in the green. If nothing else, a good snake will rattle your opponents.

Spectators:

Observers who are always around until you need someone to verify your hole-in-one.

Snake

Spoon

Spoon:

A number three wood, used for distance plus lift. Player who say he is expert with spoon speak with forked tongue.

Static cling:

Be grateful for it. When your game is lousy it's the only thing that holds you together.

Stipulated round:

Playing all 18 holes in correct sequence. Could also be a foursome of lazy attorneys. They'll stipulate to anything.

Suggestions:

You're wise if you believe only half the suggestions you get. You're a genius who shoots in the 70's if you know which half to believe.

T

Take the pipe:

To collapse under tension at a critical stage of competition. Some golfers are affected by this condition while driving to the course.

Teacher:

Club pro who has given you the best half hours of his life.

Texas wedge:

Using a putter off the green when the distance approximates Dallas to Houston.

Theories

Threesome

Theories:

Advice for improving your swing. Usually given by a friend for whom it didn't work.

Threesome:

A match in which two players alternate strokes with the same ball and oppose a single player. Golf's answer to the menage a trois.

Tournament:

A competition in either match or stroke play. Those who can play—play. Those who cannot, get a tournament named after them.

Trophy:

An award for special effort by a golfer—like a hole-in-one. An even bigger trophy should be given if he promises to stop talking about it.

Two handicap golfer:

A player with a boss who won't let him take off early, and a wife who keeps him home on weekends.

Tyro:

A young golfer who plays so well he's been offered a scholarship to medical school.

Trophy

Unplaced divot

Underachiever:

A golfer who shoots par while playing with Tom Watson.

Unplaced divot:

The golfer's version of potholes. Makes a course look like a Manhattan street.

Unplayable lie:

Cheating on your score so clumsily that nobody will play with you.

Unsolved mystery:

What happened to all the money you saved by not hiring a caddy?

Upright swing:

The club head is carried directly backward and upward from the ball, with little deviation from center. Are all you deviates paying attention?

Urinal:

Found in the men's room, the only place where nobody comes over and offers to correct your stance.

Upright swing

USGA rules:

United States Golf Association rules. There's only one thing worse than being on the wrong side of a rules argument: being on the right side when no one is listening.

Vapid:
Bland personality. A player who can walk out on an empty golf course and blend right in.

Veracity:
Conscientious morality. You still cheat on your score, but you don't enjoy it as much.

Veracity

Waste line

Waggle:

Preliminary action before hitting the ball, in which you flex the wrists and swing the club forward and backwards. The past tense of wiggle. Don't overdo the waggle. No disco dancer has ever beat Jan Stephenson.

Waistline:

If yours is 54 or more, you have to putt from memory.

Weather:

There is no way to be sure the sun will come out, but showing up at the club in hip boots, a plastic raincoat and an umbrella will certainly point things in the right direction.

Wedding anniversary:

Easy for a golfer to remember. "How could I forget? It's June 15th—on that day in 1953 I missed a two-inch putt on the 15th hole."

Whipping:

Thread or twine used to wrap the junction of the club's head and shaft. Also, featured event at the Marquis de Sade Open.

Weather

Wind cheater

Whisper:

The modulated voice of a TV golf announcer who pretends the golfer shooting on the 16th fairway can hear him in the booth at the 18th green.

Will power:

An enviable form of self control which keeps you from buying last year's polo shirts at this year's pro shop sale.

Wind cheater:

A ball hit intentionally low into the wind. If you're good enough to do this, you don't have to cheat.

Winner's share:

The pros don't share anything. Amy Alcott's golf cart has a man from Brinks riding shotgun.

X-rated:

Stories told in the locker room. Nothing is more offensive than hearing someone tell a dirty story before you can.

Yips:

Compulsive shakes that cause a player to badly miss a short putt. Only known solution for this problem is to compensate. Play courses on the San Andreas Fault and wait for a tremor.

Zinger:

A low trajectory shot aimed at an opponent's ego.